LITERACY ACROSS THE CURRICULUM Pocketbook

By Caroline Bentley-Davies

Published by:

Teachers' Pocketbooks
Laurel House, Station Approach,
Alresford, Hampshire SO24 9JH, UK
Tel: +44 (0)1962 735573
Fax: +44 (0)1962 733637
Email: sales@teacherspocketbooks.co.uk
Website: www.teacherspocketbooks.co.uk

Teachers' Pocketbooks is an imprint of Management Pocketbooks Ltd.

Series Editor – Linda Edge

This edition published 2012. Reprinted 2013.

ISBN 978 1 906610 48 7

E-book ISBN 978 1 908284 95 2

British Library Cataloguing-in-Publication Data – A catalogue record for this book is available from the British Library.

Design, typesetting and graphics by Efex Ltd. Printed in UK.

Contents

Page

Acknowledgements

With many thanks to the following people for their subject-specific expertise, assistance and invaluable advice. It is really appreciated:

Dawn German, Dan Coventry, Natalie Packer, Ross Bentley-Davies, Dennis Simms, Vanessa Lea

Foreword

'Literacy Across the Curriculum' is high on the agenda in schools. Guidance in the current Teaching Standards requires that *all* teachers should:

'Take a responsibility for promoting high standards of literacy and correct use of standard English whatever the teacher's specialism.'

One reason literacy is so important is that it enables pupils to learn and access *all* aspects of the curriculum. The ability to communicate, and to read and write effectively, maximises their chance of obtaining good qualifications (and important life skills) in all subjects – not just English.

The *Literacy Across the Curriculum Pocketbook* is for all classroom teachers and teaching assistants. It offers practical tips and guidance to help pupils improve and develop the literacy skills they need to flourish in your lessons and become successful in later life.

Foreword

This book is based on a few key premises:

1. **Literacy is important for all learning.** If pupils can read, communicate and express themselves clearly and accurately, they will succeed at school.
2. **We owe it to our pupils to help them develop their literacy.** People with high levels of literacy succeed in all aspects of life, both socially and economically. Studies show that young offenders and prisoners have particularly high levels of *illiteracy*. There is a clear link between a lack of communication skills and poor future life chances for children.
3. **Developing strategies for improving literacy across the curriculum** enhances teaching and learning across a school. Strategies do not need to be difficult. Much good practice is simple, fun and easy to implement in everyday lessons.
4. **Teachers do not have to be literacy experts** to promote literacy across the curriculum. Focusing on some aspects of literacy teaching will enhance your own knowledge and communication skills and allow you to model good practice.

Why Literacy Matters

English or LAC? What's the difference?

English and whole school literacy are clearly linked – but they are not the same thing. English teachers play a vital role in developing and teaching literacy skills such as reading expertise, writing for different purposes, spelling, punctuation and oracy.

However, English is a specific subject which includes key knowledge and skills beyond literacy, for instance: the history of the English language; knowledge of critical terminology; developing responses to a wide variety of texts, including novels, poetry and plays. In English lessons pupils are also taught how to write creatively and analyse texts.

How does 'literacy' differ? It considers the wider aspect of reading, writing and communication, the skills that need to be developed in all curriculum areas, so that pupils can manage the particular literacy demands of each subject and develop communication skills for everyday life.

Literacy is tested across the curriculum

Take a look at the question below from a recent Mathematics GCSE paper.

> Postal regulations say that for a package the length plus girth cannot exceed 108 inches or the package will not be accepted by the post office. The length is defined as the longest side of the package. The girth is defined as the measurement around the package, perpendicular to the length, ABCDA, as shown. This package is a cuboid with a length of 48 inches. Show that the greatest value for the width, w, if the package is to be accepted by the post office, is 12 inches. (2 marks)
>
> (AQA Mathematics specimen 2012, Paper 1 Q8)

Did you notice:

- The key subject-specific vocabulary that pupils need to understand?
- The amount of reading pupils need to manage for a question worth just two marks?
- General levels of vocabulary and understanding required?
- How pupils need to track, understand and shape their answers to the question?

Good literacy raises standards

Did you know that, in England, pupils gain marks for spelling, punctuation and grammar in GCSE exams other than English? In History, Religious Studies and Geography, as from Sept 2012, 5% of the marks are awarded for these aspects of writing.

Even in subjects where pupils are not marked on their accuracy, in a change to the previous exam system *all* subjects now use much longer examination questions which require students to structure and organise their extended responses. This makes significant demands on pupils' literacy skills. A sample PE GCSE paper contains the following:

> Sponsorship is very common in most sporting events, competitions and clubs. Describe, using an example, how sponsorship can be an **advantage** and help to increase participation. (3 marks)
>
> (AQA Physical Education GCSE – full course specimen paper unit 3)

Pupils need to understand the key ideas and vocabulary but they must also write (in some detail), showing they understand what is meant by the word 'describe'.

What's in it for me?

CASE STUDY

The History department realised that low level writing skills were preventing students from reaching their potential. Reviewing the mock papers they saw that pupils were unable to develop their points in sufficient detail in their written answers. They were not writing enough and their responses were poor in quality. This meant that they were losing marks.

Teachers demonstrated to pupils how to write sample answers. This involved:

- *Showing them other students' work using visualisers (equipment to electronically display sample work)*
- *Developing some writing frames (worksheets that gave opening sentences and ways of starting and structuring their responses)*
- *In marking pupils' work, indicating where they could improve and then allowing time for the improvements to be made*

Eventually, by focusing on writing skills, the History department helped their students to improve their grades.

At KS3, discussions, paired work and extensive oral work helped pupils see where they could add more detail and enabled them to rehearse their ideas verbally before they put pen to paper.

Who does what?

Improving literacy requires a clear structure and vision. There is usually a teacher in charge of literacy across the curriculum. In this book the term 'LAC Co-ordinator' will be used for that person. The table below indicates how LAC responsibilities might be arranged.

LAC Co-ordinator

- Assess whole staff LAC training needs
- Arrange / deliver training on specific areas, eg spelling, writing
- Audit current standards of literacy across the school and share information about pupil literacy levels with all staff
- Organise literacy interventions / catch-up sessions for pupils
- Adopt systems to help pupils track literacy targets
- Adopt whole school systems for marking/ spelling
- Arrange extra-curricular literacy enhancements, eg visiting authors, 'book week', competitions, awards...
- Review and chart progress; evaluate effectiveness of literacy policy

Class teachers

- Share their current knowledge of LAC with the co-ordinator
- Highlight their literacy training needs
- Adopt any whole-school policies regarding marking for literacy, teaching key words, etc
- Use displays and the environment to reinforce literacy
- Model good literacy skills in the classroom
- Teach pupils how to tackle subject - specific literacy demands as well as furthering literacy knowledge
- Make links with literacy skills in other subjects
- Promote reading for pleasure

Where to start?

In some schools there will be a clear strategic direction from your LAC Co-ordinator. The whole school might focus on a particular area – reading, for instance – for a specified amount of time. Or you might be given individual pupils' literacy targets, such as 'writing in paragraphs'. You can help to reinforce these when appropriate in your lessons. This way pupils get the opportunity to practise and embed the skills they need to learn in a number of lessons, thereby retaining the main messages.

If you are not given a lead by the LAC Co-ordinator, it is important to address literacy issues connected with your subject when they arise. So explain how to make notes, remind pupils to use paragraphs, teach key vocabulary, etc.

Similarly, you will need to identify the specific literacy challenges in your subject. Targeting a particular area, and being explicit about it in your teaching, is often the best way to start improvements.

So what *are* the literacy skills pupils need to succeed in your subject? They are interconnected and relate to three main areas… …

LAC skills

1. Oral communication

- To articulate, discuss and debate, and to use talk to develop and think through ideas
- To ask and answer questions to create 'deep' understanding
- To present and communicate formally and informally
- To organise and present ideas such as giving a presentation
- To use formal and informal speech as appropriate to the situation

2. Reading skills

- To read a range of complex texts
- To use research tools – both online and paper based
- To skim and scan for relevant information
- To review and adapt what they have read, showing understanding

3. Writing skills

- To plan, draft and review ideas
- To write and record useful notes
- To write at length, and for different purposes and audiences
- To spell, punctuate and write accurately

The remainder of this Pocketbook will help you to address your pupils' literacy skills so that they can enjoy their learning and achieve across the curriculum.

Why Literacy Matters

Speaking for Success

Vamp Up Your Vocabulary

Splendid Spelling

Raring to Read

Note Making

Write Better!

Literacy Checklist

Speaking for Success

Talk right!

The ability to communicate clearly is crucial for success, not only in school but also in later life. Gaining good employment, managing successful relationships and avoiding conflict are all due in large part to successful speaking and listening skills.

True Story

Training a group of prospective teachers, one keen would-be trainee told me he'd just been turned down for a training place. This seemed strange; he was clearly enthusiastic and had a good degree. I asked if he'd been given feedback on the reasons for this. He was told that his formal presentation skills were weak. He had also failed to make good eye contact with his audience. Verbal communication isn't easy - even for adults.

This section will explain how we can improve pupils' oracy so they can talk their way to success!

Opportunities across the school

There are many reasons to use and promote 'talk' in everyday lessons but it's worth also thinking about opportunities across the wider school environment.

Schools that develop their pupils' confidence in speaking skills often:

- Invite interesting and inspirational external speakers (this gives pupils the chance not only to hear a good speaker, but to practise formal speech by interviewing them)
- Arrange 'mock interviews' for pupils, eg as part of work experience preparation
- Involve all classes or tutor groups in researching, presenting and giving assemblies
- Have active student councils who debate and represent their peers
- Have a wide range of extra-curricular options that promote oracy

Creative ideas work well with pupils of *all* ages. Pupils need exciting, real opportunities for speaking, from reception to Year 13.

Discuss it!

All students benefit from developing their speaking skills in less formal situations. What clubs or societies does your school have that focus on oracy in an informal, fun way? Schools that develop confident speakers often have:

- Strong **Drama clubs** – not just practising plays for performance, but offering a whole range of fun 'dramatic' activities (often linked to theatre visits) to build confidence
- **Film clubs** – in the UK, the charity www.filmclub.org offers free film loans and tailored resources to promote pupil-led discussions of films and the issues they raise
- Clubs that tap into pupils' **interests**, such as: storytelling, running a school newsletter, improving the environment. These can be largely run by pupils. Some groups organise their own meetings and draw up their own organisation under the supervision of staff

You can foster interest in and awareness of more formal speech by running a debating competition for **all** tutor groups/classes. Use video clips to show good speakers and get pupils involved in preparing and practising speeches – the winners can be entered for the Rotary Youth Speaks competition.

Tutor talk

Many schools reinforce literacy by incorporating LAC activities into tutor time or registration. Using these periods to develop discussion skills is valuable for students – and a great way to find out a bit more about your tutees. You could:

- Give a talk about yourself. Then ask each tutee to prepare their own similar talk. Who knew that Tom was a prize-winning fisherman, Sandro is in a band and Fiona once lived in France? Talks can include favourite music, pictures, ideal holidays, fantasy jobs, etc
- Play word games such as 'Taboo' where pupils talk about a topic that they've recently studied without mentioning certain key words. Other pupils have to guess the topic – imagine describing photosynthesis without mentioning 'light'!
- Pupils talk about a chosen topic for 30 seconds. They mustn't repeat themselves, or say *'um'*, or use a word such as *'and'* more than three times. Start with 30 points and every time they break a rule they lose a point. The pupil with most points at the end wins

In the news

There are plenty of other fun and challenging ideas. The following is a useful way of developing knowledge of issues and news, as well as encouraging social skills:

Display the front page of a newspaper on a visualiser – or find an internet example – for five minutes so that pupils can read the 'big' international or local stories of the day. Get different pupils to read out parts of it and then give them a limited amount of time in small groups to summarise and then discuss the main aspects of it. Pupils feed back and develop a whole class discussion on the topic.

More challenge needed? Pupils adopt roles, such as chairing the discussion on their tables or acting 'in role' as one of the people in the articles. What might the manager of the factory say about the situation? How would you feel if you were a local environmentalist? Pupils can interview each other in role. Allow them to review and comment on each other's skills: would the mayor really talk like that? What is the correct level of formality for the situation?

Getting started – lesson ideas using talk

Getting pupils talking in a meaningful way helps secure learning. It means they stay on task during lessons because the learning is active and fun:

1. **Define it!** List key words or terms on red cards and their definitions on yellow. Hand them out at random. Pupils need to find their partner and discuss, or provide an example of, the definition. This is a fun, fast-paced idea for a mini plenary to check learning.
2. **Speed dating / quick info exchange.** Each pupil devises a question related to the topic they have been studying and has the answer to hand, eg *'Name an insect that tastes with its feet?* Answer: *'Butterfly / Daddy long legs.'* The class sits in two lines facing each other. They have, say, two minutes to ask and answer questions with the person opposite, testing each other and discussing responses. After two minutes one row moves along a seat. The new pairs now test each other and so on.
3. **Teach it!** Divide up revision topics and get pupils in small groups to make a presentation or design a mini lesson to teach the class key aspects of the topic in any way they like.

Say it, know it!

When you can discuss something confidently you know that you have really learnt it. Here are some ways to extend spoken contributions in class:

- Display a mind map of key words from a topic and ask pupils to discuss these with their partner, making as many connections as they can. What connections can be made? What do they know? What don't they know?
- Use the free website 'Wordle' to create arresting visual pictures from the text you paste in. Words are displayed in different sizes depending on the number of times they have been used. Pasting in a crucial scene of Macbeth, for instance, will highlight words such as *'blood'*, *'sleep'*, *'death'*. Pupils can speculate and then discuss: Which words do they expect to see? Why? What are the actual results? What can they infer from this?
- Show a clip from a topic (or film of the novel) the class have been studying but mute the sound. Pupils must devise the verbal commentary. This activity works well with science programmes or documentaries that contain lots of stills, eg history programmes with shots of artefacts, diagrams and charts. Pupils can use the visual clues to record each other, or practise their commentary and compare with the original soundtrack

Get dramatic!

Drama techniques, whether lively 'out of the seat' activities or more contained, are a great way for all subjects to promote talk and concentration. Here are a couple of ideas*:

Verbal guided descriptions
Students work in pairs, 'A' and 'B'. B's close their eyes while A's look at a picture displayed on the screen and describe it in detail to B. After five minutes, B looks and comments on how effective A's description was. This is a great activity to inspire descriptive writing in English, or as a way of reinforcing vocabulary in Modern Languages. Lively, colourful images can be readily found on the internet.

What am I?
Create stickers showing key terms, objects or people related to the topic just studied. Stick them on the students' backs. Students must ask 'yes or no questions' of different people in the room to try to discover who or what they are. Devising questions also helps promote the use of correct vocabulary, which in turn secures learning.

* For further creative and dramatic ideas see the *Drama for Learning Pocketbook*

Can you hear me?

Pupils can be keen to get their own 'air time', but less keen to let others speak – or to listen carefully when they do speak! Provide opportunities for pupils to really listen to each other:

Ask them to observe **film clips of other speakers** and lead a discussion about their skills. What makes them good or less effective communicators? Or try this small group **simulated discussion**. It's great fun and very instructive. Begin by giving pupils involved in the discussion secret roles written on cards, eg:

- **'Dominator'** – you always talk over people / interrupt
- **'Off task'** – you always mention things that are not relevant to the topic, such as TV
- **'Best friend'** – you hold no opinions of your own, just agree with the person next to you
- **'Bored person'** – you can't be bothered to pay attention
- **'All rounder'** – you listen carefully and join in appropriately

Students discuss a topic in role, eg *'Which charity should the school support this year?'* The rest of the class observes and tries to guess participants' character traits. Lead a debrief on this. What did the class observe? Let the pupils involved comment on what it was like to be in role. Use this to draw up a list of speaking and listening guidelines for tutor time / lessons.

Adapt your speech

Many pupils experience difficulty in adapting their speech for formal situations. Speaking informally when a more formal register is required creates a poor impression and can seriously disadvantage students later in life.

Katja Hall (Confederation of British Industry) explains the issue:

> 'Employers need staff to be able to, with confidence, articulate information in a clear and coherent way, to extract key details from conversation and to be ready to present a case to peers and colleagues. Leaving compulsory education without adequate spoken and communication skills is a serious blight on young people's lives and a major handicap when looking for work.'
>
> (23rd May 2012, BBC News, reported by Angela Harrison)

Pupils often speak very informally, even to their teachers, and not having many opportunities to speak in formal situations can be a real issue. How often do your students get the chance to speak formally? Arranging for people with interesting jobs to visit and give a talk to your class is a good way of creating a scenario in which students can practise formal speech. Planning and posing questions and formally thanking a visitor are key skills.

Communicating for others

Pupils are much more motivated when they are speaking for a 'real' purpose. The following work well:

- Developing inter-class activities, such as designing quizzes or competitions. These can be linked with literacy skills such as poetry-writing, or connected with wider aspects of school life, eg arranging charity events and sporting fixtures
- Older students working with younger pupils, eg as reading coaches or 'study buddies'
- Creating resources to use with younger pupils, such as story books or plays; or preparing informative presentations, for instance *'How to choose your options in Yr 9'* or *'Top tips for making your work experience a success'*, or *'How to revise for exams'*
- Class trips and activities. One school organising a trip to France had a group of pupils involved in the planning. This included making telephone calls enquiring about prices for different methods of travel and giving presentations to pupils and parents
- Linking homework with opportunities for speech, including interviewing others – perhaps for an oral history project or trialling a questionnaire for Business Studies

Using ICT to stimulate speech

Using technology is a great way of motivating pupils to talk for a real purpose and to a real audience – even if it is just their own class, and because talk is 'captured' pupils can listen to themselves. Remember, though, that you will need your headteacher's approval before any pupil work is broadcast or 'made live' beyond the classroom.

Podcasting. *'Audacity'* www.audacity.sourceforge.net/ is a free downloadable sound program that lets users record, listen to and edit their work. (You'll need access to ICT and microphones.) They can also add sounds and music for a more professional feel. Pupils might create podcasts on revision topics, to promote a school activity or to give a reading. They can listen via their phones or MP3 players to recordings made through *'Audacity'*. This can be useful for studying another language or trying to remember complex information.

Using an auto cue (having scrolling text like a newsreader) is a useful and simple way of practising public speaking or highlighting key prompts for presentations. There's a free online teleprompter at: www.CuePrompter.com. Pupils type or paste in text and the screen scrolls the words at variable speeds.

Who do you want to be today?

'Voki' is an excellent ICT tool for motivating reluctant speakers and it's very easy to use. It allows pupils (and teachers) to create a speaking avatar, or they can adopt a famous person as their mouthpiece – a past US President, for example. Pupils use a microphone to record themselves or they can type in text.

'Voki' works well for peer assessment, allowing pupils to hear each other's story openings, revision tips or ideas. It helps overcome shyness for pupils who do not want to be videoed, but whose voices need to be heard in class. It also has great potential for students learning a language. They can type in text (that has been corrected by the teacher), select the relevant language and hear it spoken with the correct intonation, accent and pronunciation. Teachers can use an avatar when giving instructions – imagine if your instructions to the class came from Dracula, a pet dog or Marie Antoinette! It's a fun way of engaging your students.

NB: As Voki is an American program, it's important that pupils ***do not*** *press the phone icon – unless they are prepared for a huge bill!*

Vamp Up Your Vocabulary

Vocabulary matters

'Vocabulary at the age of 5 is a powerful predictor of GCSE achievement.'
(Research from The Communication Trust funded by the DFE.)

Pupils face a huge range of complex subject-specific words that they need to learn and understand. They also need to grow their 'word power'. Pupils who use a range of varied and interesting vocabulary are successful communicators who can articulate their views – verbally and in writing – with flair and interest.

The youngest children depend on their teachers and parents to introduce and help them discover new words and their meanings. If you make learning new words fun and interesting you will keep pupils engaged, whatever their age. This section will give you practical ideas for improving pupils' vocabulary and securing subject-specific terminology.

Level Up

It is important to encourage pupils to use more interesting and sophisticated vocabulary. If they simply recycle the limited number of words they already know, their writing and expression can be lacklustre – it needs to sparkle to engage the audience.

One teacher uses an activity she calls *'Level Up'* to improve her classes' vocabulary. She writes a pedestrian word or sentence on the board and gives pupils five minutes to improve it. Pupils then share and discuss each other's improvements, using a thesaurus and dictionary to check definitions and ensure that words are used correctly.

> *'Jamie's house was large, but his bedroom was dark and small.'*

becomes:

> *'Jamie's house was palatial, but his bedroom was dingy and cramped.'*

Now, all this teacher needs to say to her pupils is *'level up'* and they know they need to enhance their vocabulary.

Wrong words

One secondary teacher recently admitted to me, *'I don't like pupils to experiment with new vocabulary because they often use a word in the wrong context and it doesn't make sense.'*

This will happen but pupils won't ultimately improve their vocabulary range or deepen their understanding unless they are allowed to make errors.

One boy, writing about the Middle Ages and trying out a new word, wrote that most people were pheasants in the 1300s! He was encouraged to look up 'pheasant' and then corrected it to 'peasant'. He was then asked to think about how he could remember the difference between the two words. He concluded that pheasants (beginning with the 'f' sound) had 'f'eathers.

By the end of the exercise he had used a dictionary and secured two new words.

Getting creative

Sometimes you want pupils to really reflect on **why** a writer has used a particular word. An effective activity is to remove some of the interesting words from a piece of text.

Below is the opening of a piece of persuasive writing encouraging people to book a holiday. Several key words have been removed:

> *Come to sunny Wales for a __________ holiday. Nestling in the Welsh countryside is a ___________ holiday cottage, equipped with all the luxuries you need for a perfect and ____________ holiday.*

After reading the text, pupils must individually note down words they think would work well in the gaps. Their choices can then be discussed: which words worked best and why? The full original text can then be revealed and vocabulary choices discussed and compared.

This is a great activity for encouraging pupils to think about individual words. Why does *'relaxing'* sound better than *'quiet'*? Why is *'quaint'* more appealing than *'old'*? It can be used with any type of text and really helps pupils think about their word choices.

Varying vocabulary

Developing pupils' interest in words and so expanding their vocabulary is best achieved by making it part of each lesson, tackling and dealing with words when they occur, rather than having separate 'vocabulary lessons'.

Good practice includes:

- Encouraging pupils to try out new words and look up their meanings to check that they are using them correctly
- Having plenty of dictionaries and thesauruses on hand in classrooms

Think about issuing guidance, or even selling dictionaries and thesauruses, on parents' evenings. If pupils are used to referring to them in class and have their own copies, they will use them for homework too, increasing both word power and independence.

Remember, pupils with iPads and kindles can download free dictionaries and thesauruses. E-readers have a tool which gives the definition of any word you hover over.

New words

There is sometimes a tendency to 'dumb down' reading material for pupils. Rather than watering down difficult texts we need to help pupils master tricky words.

- Ask if they know the meanings of unfamiliar words in a text – don't assume that they do. Encourage them to predict meaning and to check it
- Have somewhere to display new words, maybe a special *'words of the week'* board, or perhaps section off parts of the whiteboard
- Allow pupils to practise and experiment with speaking, spelling and writing new words. Knowing how to pronounce words correctly increases confidence about using them
- Ask pupils to investigate and explore words from the real world. Encourage them to discuss and discover new words
- Give plenty of praise for those who take a chance and try out a new word

Four key principles

There are four things to bear in mind when teaching vocabulary:

1. It is most effective when taught on a regular basis. The best teachers explain and enhance vocabulary each lesson.
2. Always aim to 'skill up' pupils rather than 'dumb down' the vocabulary in your lessons.
3. Practice makes perfect. Reinforce new learning by giving pupils the opportunity to practise, make mistakes and learn from them before the word is secured.
4. You may need to add to and extend your own vocabulary – we are always learning!

When it comes to helping pupils master your subject's specific or technical vocabulary there are plenty of fun ways to achieve your goal. Read on for some of the most effective teaching tips, tools and techniques.

1. The vocabulary ladder

Teaching subject-specific words can be challenging. One way to begin is by thinking about the rungs on the vocabulary ladder.

1. What are the most challenging or difficult words in the topic you will be teaching?
2. Make sure that you have a list of them – and check that their spelling is correct in your notes and that they appear accurately in displays and worksheets.
3. How you will introduce them? What strategies do you personally use to remember them?
4. Praise pupils for their efforts to use correct terminology – if they make mistakes help them to correct themselves.
5. Ensure that pupils record the correct spelling and definition – some schools use different colour pens for this or allocate parts of their books for key terms.
6. Check and reinforce pupils' knowledge by getting them to use the words in a real context – perhaps get them involved in a test or game.
7. New vocabulary is secured.

2. Make it memorable

When teaching complex new vocabulary, think about ways to help pupils remember these new terms. **Mnemonics** can make important aspects of a word, or even the spelling, memorable.

Start by sharing your own knowledge – what helps *you* learn? Helping pupils to make up their own mnemonics will make the learning stick. Encouraging your class to compete in devising mnemonics to sort out common errors can make difficult ideas fun.

In subjects such as Science where difficult terms need to be learnt in a correct order, mnemonics are invaluable, eg the hierarchical organisation of life will always spring to mind if pupils learn that:

King Philip came over for greasy sausages	=	**K**ingdom **P**hylum **C**lass **O**rder **F**amily **G**enus **S**pecies

Similarly, tricky spellings can suddenly become straightforward with a clever mnemonic. Who will forget how to spell 'ne**c**e**ss**ary' when they link it to a shirt with 'one **c**ollar and two **s**leeves'?

3. Weave a web of words

Helping pupils understand patterns and word groups is an effective way of expanding their word power. If they learn that certain prefixes mean certain things, then teaching them a few can help them decipher and build up a wide vocabulary that can transfer to other studies.

Complex scientific words can be baffling, but teaching a tiny number of Latin or Greek roots will help your pupils build up a personal lexicon.

The word *'polysaccharide'*, for example, looks complicated, but once pupils learn that *'poly'* means 'many' and *'saccharide'* means 'sugar', it's a small step to seeing that *'polysaccharide'* means: 'many molecules bonded in a chain to make sugars'.

Learning the prefix *'poly'* helps with many other words: *'polygons'* in maths (a many-sided shape), or *'polygamy'* or *'polytheistic'* in RE (marrying more than one partner and believing in more than one God).

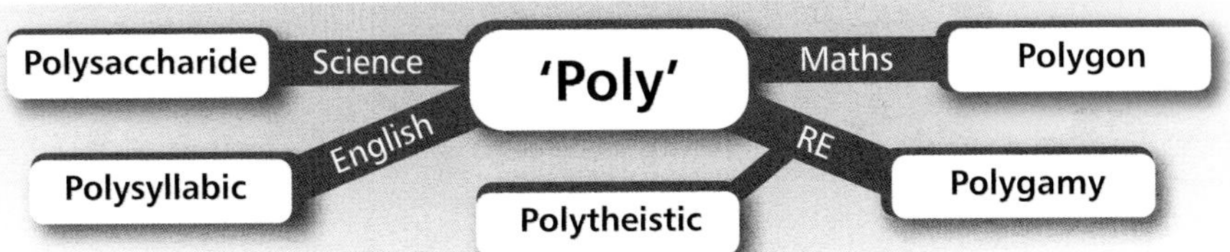

4. Webs on the wall

Using your classroom wall to display and build wall webs is a fun and highly visual way to show pupils how word meanings connect. Start with displaying a prefix connected to your topic. Get pupils to add to and develop the wallweb using dictionaries and their notes, eg:

'Photo' means 'signifying light'. Add in *'synthesis'*. This means 'to make things'. So *'photo'* + *'synthesis'* means 'light to make things'.

Photograph	=	light + pictures
Photophobia	=	light + fear of
Photosensitive	=	affected by light

Just teaching pupils one prefix and exploring it can both develop their subject-specific knowledge – in this case science – and widen their general vocabulary.

Photograph — **Photo** — **?**

Photophobia — **Photosensitive** — **Photochromic**

5. Look it up!

Having good reference dictionaries on hand in all classrooms is a great way to help pupils investigate and take an interest in words. The choice of dictionary will be dependent upon the ages and abilities of the pupils you teach.

Suitable dictionaries for secondary schools/ Key Stage 2 include: *Collins new School Dictionary* or *Oxford Dictionary for Schools*. Look for a dictionary that includes the origins of words. Pupils can then investigate words and understand how they are connected, thus building up their word power.

www.oxforddictionaries.com has lots of dictionary ideas, interesting vocabulary information, and suggestions for teaching pupils about words. The *'children's and schools dictionary selector page'* shows age-specific pages from different dictionaries. There is good access to online dictionaries and helpful tips on how to use them.

Encourage pupils to record new words by starting their own dictionaries in the back of their exercise books. This can be linked with spelling – see page 32 for an example of how a school incorporates a dictionary with spelling practice.

6. Repeat, repeat, repeat

Recording words is important, but it's not enough to cement the learning. Repetition is a key strategy for embedding new vocabulary – it is thought that we need to hear and reflect on new knowledge five different times to secure it.

Mini tests at the start of a lesson are helpful. Try a **'quick ten quiz'**, with ten questions linked to words pupils have met in their studies. This hooks students into the lesson and reinforces learning from the previous lesson.

But teaching vocabulary needs to be fresh and interesting to keep pupils on their toes. By using games to secure new vocabulary you can repeat and reinforce while exciting and enthusing your pupils about language.

Have you tried Key Word Pictionary, Vocabulary Bingo or Spot the Word Difference? Read on!

7. Key Word Pictionary

In the classic Pictionary game the aim is for a person to draw a word so that their partner can guess it. In school, Pictionary can be used to reinforce understanding. It's an ideal plenary or revision activity lasting 5-15 minutes maximum.

1. Create at least 15 cards with key terms / vocabulary on them, eg: *'VAT', 'sole trader', 'limited company', 'profit', 'cash flow',* etc. You can laminate them for future reference.
2. Divide class into groups of 4 to form 2 teams of 2 people. Give each group a set of cards.
3. One person in each team looks at the word or term on the first card and both draw it (without using words or symbols). Their respective team mates have to guess what it is.
4. The team who gets it right first gains a point and a further point for giving the definition. You could award a bonus point for spelling the answer correctly. Pupils take turns to draw until all the cards are gone – the winning team has the most points.

How would you draw: *'arable farming'/ 'personification'/ 'prime numbers'/ 'transubstantiation'* or a *'crustacean'*? Pens to the ready for a fun and memorable way to reinforce vocabulary!

8. Vocabulary bingo

Vocabulary bingo is another favourite for consolidating understanding of technical terms, or reinforcing new vocabulary. It works well at the end of a unit / topic.

1. You need to have taught a range of technical terms and their definitions – ideally at least 15 – and have given pupils time to learn them, perhaps for homework.
2. You can make and laminate bingo cards for future use, or just ask pupils to draw a large five by five grid. List on the board all of the vocabulary under consideration.
3. Ask pupils to copy them randomly on to their grids.
4. You also need slips of paper, each containing a definition. When you pull a slip of paper from the hat and read out the definition, pupils must tick off or place a counter on the matching term on their grids. Walk round the room to check it's being done correctly.
5. Pupils who get a line of answers first are the winners.
6. Issue rewards and take time to clarify meanings and misconceptions.

9. Spot the word difference

We may think we have taught our students the key words, but we only really know if they've understood and learnt them when we hear or see that they can use them correctly.

A simple but effective way of testing key vocabulary is to play 'odd one out':

Display three words and ask pupils to consider which is the odd one out. This gets them thinking critically and reflectively about not just the words' meanings but their links with other words and topics. Sometimes there might be a clear 'right' answer, other times the discussion is more important. For example:

Which is the odd one out?

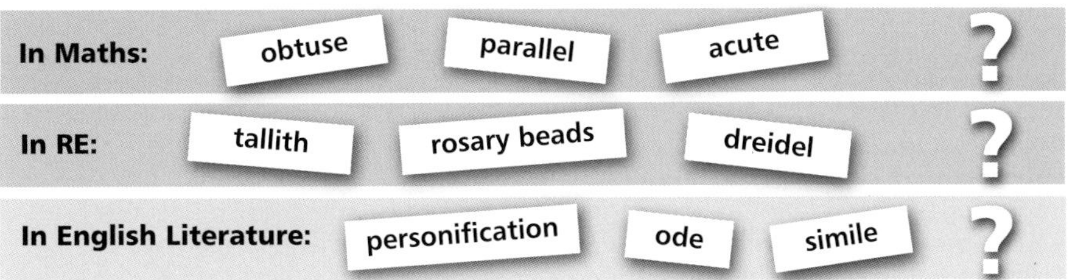

10. Running dictation

This technique is often used by MFL teachers who have to teach an immense amount of new vocabulary, but it can be easily adapted for other subjects.

1. The teacher affixes a piece of text to the wall.
2. Pupils work in small relay teams. One pupil gets a minute to go up to and study the text on the wall and then return to tell their team what it says. The team has to scribe it / translate it.
3. After a couple of minutes or so another pupil 'runs' up and returns.

Pupils work together to complete the text as a whole. The aspect of competition makes it exciting. Prizes can be awarded to the winners.

To adapt this task for other subject areas make sure it is sufficiently challenging – for example not just 'copying out' the text. In an English lesson you could have a dull description which your pupils need not only to remember but to 'pep up' by improving the vocabulary. In Science the 'text' could be a complicated scientific process which pupils have to draw or present as a labelled diagram thereby transferring the knowledge and securing it.

11. Loop cards

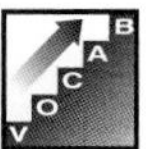

Loop cards are a great way of checking at the end of a topic that your class know and understand the key terms. They also ensure that **all** pupils are alert and engaged.

Hand out a card to every pupil. One end of the card has a key piece of vocabulary and the other end has a definition – of a **different** word.

All pupils stand up. One pupil reads out their key word and all pupils check to see who has the definition. The pupil with the correct definition reads it out. Then that pupil gives their key term and pupils respond again with the right definition.

Key word:

Protein

Definition:

This is an illness caused by a deficiency in vitamin C.

This works as pupils listen intently a) so they don't miss their turn and b) to see if the answers are correct. The repetition helps memory, and the speed with which pupils answer indicates their level of confidence.

12. Over to you

Getting pupils to 'test' each other is a very good way of involving them actively in learning key vocabulary. Making up questions and providing answers is challenging!

You can draw up various question stems to spark off ideas or just give pupils several answers connected with the topic. Suppose that in History you have been studying the 1920s – Wall Street Crash, Prohibition, Isolationism, Roosevelt, The Depression, etc. Dish out handfuls of these 'answers' to each student.

Give them a time limit during which they must circulate, giving other pupils an answer and waiting for them to think of an appropriate question to match. If their 'partner' gives an appropriate response, they are given a tally point on their score card. They are then given a second 'answer' to come up with a question for. If the question is wrong, the roles swap. Students need to 'collect' as many right answers to questions (or rather, questions to answers!) as possible. The winner has the fullest score card.

At the end of the lesson the hardest and most challenging questions can be discussed with the group, and strategies for learning these words can be devised.

Why Literacy Matters

Speaking for Success

Vamp Up Your Vocabulary

Splendid Spelling

Raring to Read

Note Making

Write Better!

Literacy Checklist

Splendid Spelling

Get set, spell!

Teaching key words effectively really helps pupils with spelling. Remember, children often pick an unadventurous word that they can spell, rather than trying an exciting vocabulary choice, for fear of misspelling. If we want pupils to say that the ride was *'exhilarating'* rather than just *'good'* we need to boost their confidence in spelling. Being a good speller isn't a gift – we can all improve!

Stop Take time to discuss words with your class. Are they clear about the meaning?

Look Consider the letter order and what the word looks like on the page. How is it put together? Are there words within the word or any patterns?

Listen Students learn most effectively when explaining concepts and ideas to each other. Get them to talk about how they will learn the word. What ideas can they come up with to fix it in their memory?

Go Experiment with using the word. Did they get it right? Allow them time to reflect and review their learning.

Spelling rules

Many of us remember the spelling rule we chanted at school *'i before e except after c'*. We may have found it helpful in learning how to spell words like 'believe' and deceive' but, as with many other 'helpful' spelling rules, there are plenty of exceptions. Words like: 'height', 'feign', 'weight', 'seize', 'sleight', 'deign', etc don't follow the rule.

Adopting spelling rules wholesale is problematic! The English Language is complex and spelling issues can be very individual.

This section will focus on different strategies for helping pupils tackle tricky words. (If you are very keen to know more about spelling rules your literacy co-ordinator may recommend resources, or speak to the English Department, who are often the spelling ninjas of the school!)

Tricky words

The spelling of some words is just very tough to learn. Showing pupils that it takes a bit of time and effort is key. Taking a few minutes to explain how **you** learn difficult words is a good way of showing that it doesn't just happen by magic.

It is also crucial for students to see that, even as a teacher, you need to reflect on, review and check your spelling.

Consider the notoriously tricky word *'onomatopoeia'*, a technical term used in English language to identify those words that sound like their meaning – eg *'crash', 'smash', 'bang'*.

Many pupils (and some teachers!) find the letter order very difficult to remember. Spending a few minutes discussing the word (and similarly tricky ones) with the class is helpful. What strategies will you use to help you recall the correct spelling?

Tricky words

Strategies for fixing the word in the memory need to be active and dynamic. If you can make them fun and reward pupils for coming up with ideas themselves, then they will be engaged in the process and make progress. After all, we all remember what has attracted our attention.

With 'onomatopoeia' you might:

- Look at the words within the word such as 'on', 'mat', etc
- Discuss it and demonstrate writing it
- Trace it with fingers (this can help secure the word in your memory)
- Use rhyme or song (some pupils will come up with really creative ideas)
- Draw pictures or posters highlighting letters

Some people also learn effectively by moulding plasticine shapes or drawing fun pictures to embed the word in their mind. Different pupils learn in different ways. Most students will be helped by methods that use sight, sound or touch, or a combination of these.

Subject-specific spellings

Most subjects have a range of words that pupils typically misspell. English teachers tire of constantly correcting 'dairy' entries and **all** subjects have their own 'troublesome' words that pupils persistently get wrong.

It is worth thinking about **how** this can be addressed both in lessons and at home.

LAC Co-ordinators might like to ask subjects to nominate key words that pupils misspell or misunderstand per Year Group, so that these can be compiled into displays or listed in a spelling section of the homework diary.

Pupils can be set homework to learn these key words. Having them listed in the homework diary encourages parents / carers to make use of them with pupils. Some subjects might also get pupils to create a *subject glossary* in the back of their exercise books, so that they are also compiling the meanings of words.

Make spellings stick

Here are some ways to make spellings stick:

- Classroom displays. Students can create their own imaginative displays of challenging words. This not only helps fix the correct spelling in their minds, it also livens up the classroom walls
- Set challenges and tasks inviting pupils to invent memorable ways of remembering troublesome spellings
- Use individual mini whiteboards as a way of quickly testing and checking spelling accuracy – **all** pupils hold up their answers so you can easily see the results and take time to address common problems
- In active lessons like PE getting pupils to chant or bounce the ball as they spell out the letters can be fun!

Talking about it

Have rich discussions about the meanings of words rather than just testing them. One friend's primary aged daughter could spell 'combustion', 'impeccable', 'chamber maid' and 'irrational' in a spelling test, but had no idea what they meant!

Regular spelling tests help to secure learning and ensure that pupils commit words to memory, but selecting words that are connected to the topic which is being studied, and that pupils understand is a much better solution than testing random words.

Remember, too, that even if pupils can memorise words for a test, they won't necessarily remember the spelling two weeks later. Allow time for pupils to re-visit their learning.

Teaching and transforming spelling

When correcting pupils' work make a note of words or word groups that people have struggled with so that you can address them next lesson. Delivering a micro teaching session is good practice and need only take a few minutes. It can be more effective than repeatedly correcting the same spellings in their books. This is particularly true of homophones (words that sound the same, but have different meanings and spellings) and plurals. Notorious homophones include: there/ their/ they're; witch/ which; bare/ bear; meet/ meat; serial/ cereal.

Sometimes writing the correction and getting the pupil to write another sentence including the word can be useful.

If you notice pupils are making mistakes take a few minutes to get them involved in thinking about **how** they will learn, remember and master a word's correct spelling.

CASE STUDY

In GCSE, PE students were confusing 'weight' and 'wait' in their written work. The teacher asked them to come up with ideas for remembering which was which. They agreed that 'weight' is related to heaviness – it is a longer and therefore heavier word than 'wait'. Teaching spelling like this is fun and it makes the learning memorable.

Taking responsibility – total recall

Most pupils will also face individual challenges with their spellings. In these cases teachers should identify and often correct the spelling in their written work. However, it is vital that pupils take responsibility for learning that spelling and a spelling log is one way of doing this.

The most effective sequence for this learning is:

1. Pupils record the correct spelling of a word in their log.
2. They learn it using: **Look, Say, Cover, Write** (or trace), **Check**.
3. Pupils need to practise this (at least five times) or write it in a new sentence.
4. They can be tested by their peers / teacher / parent / tutor.

Hopefully the correct spelling is now secured!

It is important to have a written record of this process so that the spelling can be checked and tested by the teacher or teaching assistant.

Little and often

Many parents are keen to help their children with spellings. Make sure they realise that mammoth spelling sessions can be very disheartening and ineffective for pupils' learning. Short but very regular 'bursts', even as short as five or ten minutes a day, are better for building and improving skills.

Involving parents in helping to 'test' and check spellings for homework can be invaluable. Using a spelling log like the one on the next page is an effective strategy. Some pupils will copy down the spelling incorrectly, so active ways of learning spellings with friends, teaching assistants and parents is a good way of checking that the word is correct – before it is committed to memory.

Spelling Log

Correct spelling	Meaning	1st attempt	2nd attempt	3rd attempt	4th attempt	5th attempt	Signed off
isle	An island	isale	isle	isle	isle	isle	[signature]
current	Flow in the river	currant	Current	current	current	current	[signature]
plantation	Area of land where crops are grown, eg cotton	plantation	plantation				

Struggling spellers

Some pupils will experience considerable problems with spelling because of individual learning difficulties. Your school SENCO will have detailed information on individual pupils' learning needs and will be able to share effective learning strategies. If you are teaching pupils with dyslexia or for whom English is an additional language, see also the *Dyslexia Pocketbook* and *EAL Pocketbook*.

Whilst it is vital to help pupils become accurate spellers, it is also important not to dishearten them by correcting every single spelling mistake. Getting work back from your teacher that is full of spelling corrections can lead to great anxiety. It is important to draw attention to other aspects of pupils' work so they realise that spelling is only one component of successful writing.

Literacy marking policy

In schools where literacy skills are valued there is a clear, whole-school marking policy. The best policies are developed with reference to a range of different staff and incorporate good practice from across the school. They give **explicit guidance** and promote **consistency of approach**. Good policies will have a positive effect on literacy levels across the school. They should be referred to, reviewed and updated on a regular basis.

So what might you find in your whole-school policy? Typically:

- You will not be seeking to correct every single spelling error (correcting everything is soul-destroying for weaker pupils). Instead, pick out key words or look for patterns of errors
- There will be agreed, common abbreviations for corrections
- There will be guidance on how pupils should act on your corrections
- There will be common mechanisms for tracking targets and recording vocabulary and spellings

Make sure you are familiar with your school's marking policy and that you follow its guidance.

Reading and spelling

Reading, whether it's books, magazines, online resources or other printed text, helps some, but not all, pupils with their spelling. (We can all cite highly competent readers who are weak spellers.) Exposure to correct spelling is one way of reinforcing accuracy. In school ensure that:

- Time is given to allow and promote individual reading opportunities
- Displays in classrooms promote correct spellings (you can make corrections in pencil so as not to detract too much from the presentation)
- Before pupils start work, 'mind map' with your class the key vocabulary they might need, paying attention to correct spelling
- Key words connected with the topic are on display so pupils can refer to them

Some classes use 'word mats' – laminated sheets with key words, spellings and checklists that pupils can refer to while they work.

Spelling bees, games and competitions

Spelling can be fun! *'See spelling as a challenge rather than a chore'* is a good mantra.

1. Why not run a '**spelling bee**' competition where pupils learn a range of spellings that increase in complexity in successive rounds? It can be organised within the school or across schools and gives status and prestige to being able to spell. *The Times* newspaper runs a national spelling bee which attracts over 1,200 schools in the UK. Although this is clearly an activity enjoyed by the most able spellers, www.timesspellingbee.co.uk has some fun games and resources for spellers of all levels. 4.5 million spelling games have been played on it!

2. Pupils of all abilities really enjoy the board game **Scrabble** and the word game **'Bananagrams'**. Both require focus on vocabulary and accurate spelling. Some schools have set up lunch-time Scrabble and / or Bananagrams clubs. The competitive nature of the games encourages players to 'check up' on words in dictionaries to ensure that their friends / opponents are using real, accurately spelt words.

Raring to Read

Reading matters

'Too many children in England do not read or write well enough by the time they leave primary school.' (Reading by Six: How the best schools do it. Ofsted, 2010)

The ability to read is one of the most important life skills we gain from education. Pupils need to do more than just understand what they have read: they need to appreciate and enjoy reading, so that it enriches their life and is a source of pleasure. In 'red hot reading schools':

- All teachers see promoting reading as part of their role and know how to highlight reading skills explicitly in lessons
- Links between the library and teachers are well developed and all staff recommend books, resources and stock
- Quality time is given for stimulating reading activities
- There is a range of author visits / activities designed to excite interest
- Pupils are surveyed about what could make reading better
- There are effective strategies to promote reading at home

This chapter looks at some of the barriers to developing reading expertise. It suggests ideas for promoting reading for enjoyment across the school and offers practical classroom strategies for reading development, applicable across the age and subject range.

Developing good readers

In developing successful readers we're aiming for pupils who:

- Can read and 'decode' text (ie use their understanding of sounds and letters to correctly read words)
- Are confident readers who enjoy books and reading
- Can use a range of reading skills to develop good study habits, eg: skimming, scanning, reading lengthy texts, finding out information, etc
- Develop and can use high level reading skills – reading between the lines and inferring
- Can use their reading skills and knowledge of texts to improve their writing skills. They can imitate other writers, make notes, understand how writers organise their ideas, etc

Pupils who struggle to read will struggle in all areas of the curriculum.

Teaching reading skills

Primary schools in the UK teach children to read using synthetic phonics. Some secondary schools teach 'catch up sessions' for those who have not secured the crucial de-coding skills. Teaching phonics is beyond the remit of this Pocketbook; however good quality phonics teaching is characterised by the following:

- High quality regular and systematic sessions for pupils
- Good modelling and accurate pronunciation by the teacher / support staff
- Interactive sessions that get **all** pupils really involved in what they are learning, such as tracing the letters
- A close system of tracking pupils' progress so that success can be recorded and interventions made

Tip: A useful application for checking pronunciation is *'Mr Phonics'*. Available from www.mrthorne.com, it shows an enthusiastic teacher – Mr Thorne – demonstrating and explaining phonics.

Reader issues

> 'Reading for pleasure is the most important indicator of the future success of a child' (OECD, 2002).

However recent research suggests that some pupils are reading less than ever before:

> 'In 2005 1 in 10 young people surveyed by the Literacy Trust said they did not have a book at home, while in 2011 the figure is 1 in 3. With one in six people having the literacy level expected of an eleven year old this is of great concern'.
>
> (The Gift of Reading – National Literacy Trust.)

There is also evidence to suggest that certain groups seem to read less than others and need particular encouragement. These include boys, particularly white working class boys, and children from deprived backgrounds.

Pupils these days read various online texts and have become used to reading 'bitesize' blogs and webpages. Online resources can be very appealing, but pupils need also to develop 'reading stamina' so that they can confidently tackle sustained texts, whether online or in 'hard copy'. Many schools are tapping into the motivating factor of electronic resources, buying e-readers and iPads to encourage wider reading of whole texts.

How hard is it?

If you know your pupils' current reading ages, you can differentiate accordingly. Imagine having a reading age of 7 and being expected to understand RE worksheets that require a reading age of 13. What could be more demotivating?

- Do you have information about the reading ages of your pupils? (This will usually be available from the SENCO / Literacy Co-ordinator)
- Do you reflect on the reading material you use? How do pupils cope with it?
- Do you explore difficult vocabulary before sharing a resource with a class?

There are various free online testers that can work out, according to length and complexity of sentences and vocabulary, how demanding the text you are expecting pupils to read is. Try the SMOG calculator www.niace.org.uk/mis/smogcalculator

Of course, to improve pupils' reading levels we do need to stretch and challenge them. Don't shy away from using challenging texts with struggling readers; just be aware of the implications of doing so. Setting a homework that requires a high reading age just to understand the instructions might prevent the homework being completed; whereas looking at a harder text in class, discussing difficult words and explaining reading strategies before you start can pre-empt potential problems.

Top tips for creating reading materials

Whatever subject you teach, when you are writing a worksheet, or presenting or displaying other reading material, consider:

- The layout – text that is too dense can be physically difficult to read
- Paragraphing and clear headings – they can help make the topic clear
- Fonts – avoid using too many. Choose a font that is easy to read such as **Comic Sans**. Too much going on in a text can be very distracting for some readers
- Paper colour – printing on dark paper or using coloured ink can obscure the letters. Equally, some readers find very white paper creates a distracting glare. Dyslexic students often find text easier to read if it is on yellow paper
- Pupils with dyslexia prefer sans–serif fonts such as **Arial** and **Verdana**. There are no distracting 'tails' at the end of strokes to obscure the shape of the letters

Questions to engage

Whenever you are using a text with pupils, it is good practice to be explicit about the reading skills involved, whether it is a website in Media Studies, an examination paper in Maths, a historical document in History, or a report in Business Studies.

Great practice in teaching reading involves posing good questions that encourage pupils to think about the text before they start reading in detail:

- What do they notice when they quickly *skim* over it?
- Give them five minutes to pre-read part of a text – get them to note down or talk to their partner about what they notice. What questions does it raise?
- Explore characteristics of the text. How do you know it is a newsletter / story / persuasive leaflet / web page? What conventions are used? What does the title suggest? What intrigues you as a reader?
- Are any words unfamiliar? Get them to predict possible meaning from the context and the words around them
- Encourage them to look up unfamiliar words and add them to their word bank

Model it

Pupils learn from us; we are their role models. Demonstrate and talk through how you approach a text so that pupils can see your thought processes. This helps them to understand that reading is a dynamic process requiring thinking and reflection. Involve your class: get them to reflect on what you are doing, rather than just telling them.

To make pupils aware of different reading strategies and when they are appropriate, we also need to model:

- **Skimming** through a text (getting general ideas about it)
- **Scanning** for particular words or ideas and
- **Using an index**

Make it active

I once thought I had independent reading cracked – all my pupils appeared to be quietly engrossed in their books. After congratulating myself, I asked one boy, Sam, at the end of the lesson about the novel he was reading:

'Problem is, Miss, with me - reading is just in one eye and out the other.'

He had sat quietly 'reading' all lesson, but couldn't talk meaningfully about what he had read. This was a wake-up call for me – pupils who sit in silence apparently 'reading' aren't always getting a lot out of it.

Of course, we need to develop pupils' private reading and allow them time to read, but Sam taught me an important lesson: I needed to make reading 'stick'. Sam could read the words on the page but he wasn't managing any higher level skills, such as evaluating or considering what he was reading. I needed to raise my game!

Make it stick

There are many ways to make reading stick – whether it's private reading or reading together in class. These include good **interactive questioning** by the teacher and a host of **interactive teaching strategies**.

When pupils are reading get them to think and design some 'big' questions that require them to be 'active readers'. These can be displayed on the board or wall, or made into individual bookmarks so pupils can easily refer to them:

- What am I finding out?
- Are there any words I don't understand?
- How do I feel about this text?
- Are there any words/ phrases/ descriptions I particularly noticed or like/ dislike?
- How would I explain what I have read to somebody else?
- What do I think will happen next?

Giving pupils time to discuss these questions with their partner and encouraging them to feed back their ideas is one way of making reading much more active.

Active reading with DARTS

Instead of worksheets, try the following DARTS (directed activities related to texts). They are simple, but invaluable ways to make reading active:

- Use highlighter pens to underline key words and important points.
- Think of three questions they want to ask about the text.
- Re-arrange the text in the correct order (provide it in cut up strips).
- Spend three minutes talking to their neighbour about what they have learnt.
- Remove some key words so pupils have to think about these and what they might add.
- Remove the subheadings and titles – pupils have to write their own.
- Get pupils to represent the new information in a diagram/picture.

Teachers who use DARTS activities report that pupils are more engaged and better able to talk about what they have read.

Motivating reluctant readers

Whilst we want to encourage 'private reading', the following can motivate reluctant readers who won't gain anything from sitting silently with a book:

Group reading – giving a small group of 4/5 pupils the same novel to read. Several publishers produce little booklets of ideas that can be used with group readers. Oxford University Press 'Roller-coaster Series', Pearson 'Heroes' series or NATE's group and guided reading materials are all popular novels or plays with reading guidance. Pupils enjoy reading in turns and discussing ideas.

Reading aloud – reluctant readers (often boys), enjoying reading drama scripts aloud. Oxford University Press have some exciting ones, including gothic plays and some based on popular novels, such as 'War Horse'. They are motivating because all pupils get a speaking part and so get involved.

Using e-books and audio – many school libraries stock audio books which pupils enjoy reading along to or just listening to. UK public libraries offer free downloads of a massive range of e-books that can be read on PCs, some e-readers and some portable devices such as iPods. Schools who make links with local libraries can often make use of these free resources after pupils have visited and been issued with a local library card.

Developing a reading culture in school

If pupils enjoy reading they'll do it more often, and the more they read the more likely they are to become highly capable readers. In this fast-paced, highly technical world there are many more pastimes that might appear more obviously exciting competing for pupils' attention. It is up to us to make 'em want to read!

Schools with a thriving reading culture:

- Ensure that there is a range of plentiful, attractive, up-to-date reading books and resources – including electronic readers, such as iPads, kindles etc which can be purchased already pre-loaded with texts and useful apps
- Provide regular designated time for reading and opportunities to renew books
- Share good ideas for recommended books / resources from staff and other pupils
- Involve other staff – not just the English teachers and school librarians in promoting reading and developing a 'buzz' about reading
- Track and monitor pupils' reading and reading habits so it is clear what is working and what might be improved. Stocking magazines, graphic novels and up-to-date non-fiction is a good way to encourage pupils to visit the school library

Keeping on track – records and rewards

What methods do you use to help pupils keep track of their reading? Children love being rewarded for their reading. Many schools use 'Reading Logs' or 'Reading Records' where pupils chart their progress. They select from a range of tasks to review aspects of their reading, such as response journals, jacket designs, comments on characters, reviews or recommendations, etc. Don't just refer to them in literacy-based lessons; they are an excellent discussion opportunity – all pupils like teachers to take an interest in what they do.

Children and teenagers often 'get stuck' reading a very limited range of authors. Completing a record can be one way of encouraging them to try a wider range, particularly if rewards are offered for reading a range of genres.

You can download a simple reading record to print on to coloured card from www.bentley-davies.co.uk Or if you have a budget for a professional-looking reading log it's worth getting hold of some of the wonderful *'Rooted in Reading'* Passports produced by CFBT, available from www.nate.org.uk. These colourful resources are motivating and attractive for readers of all ages.

Tip: Did you know one of the biggest factors in encouraging pupils to read is other pupils' recommendations?

Special events and reading celebrations

Does your school celebrate reading by holding 'special' events, hosting reading weeks or World Book Day celebrations (1st March). Do you get involved? These 'one off' events promote the fun that can be had with reading and really inspire pupils.

It is important for pupils to see that reading is valued and enjoyed by all staff in school. One school even had the lunchtime supervisors involved in the reading events.

Activities can include:

- Competitions – including pub-style quizzes held in the library; 'famous first line' competitions; 'finding out' challenges, such as matching the teacher with their favourite literary character
- Lunchtime readings / reading assemblies – staff from different subjects (including the headteacher) provide short readings from their favourite childhood books
- Readathon (a fun way to promote reading and raise money for charity) www.readathon.org
- Challenging able readers to shadow the www.Carnegiegreenaway.org.uk shortlist. Pupils read books shortlisted for Carnegie / Greenaway medals and vote for their favourite

Do you read me?

Meeting a writer can be a life-changing experience for some pupils. Showing them a real example of somebody making their living from writing and reading is incredibly motivating.

Check out **The National Centre for Language and Literature (University of Reading)** www.ncll.reading.ac.uk for a list of authors who visit schools. Even better, ask other schools for recommendations. Think about whether you want the author to address a large group, run a writer's workshop or stage a question and answer session. Make the most of it by:

- Doing some pre-visit preparation – pupils can research the author, read examples of their work and prepare questions to ask on the day
- Using the visit as a 'way in' to studying the author, so ensure that his / her books are displayed in the library
- Starting up a writing / reading club inspired by these visits. Perhaps run a competition to write a short story in a similar genre? (Ask if the writer will be a judge)
- Taking the opportunity for pupils to write a formal thank you letter post-visit

Pairs and buddies

If pupils don't enjoy reading they are more likely to give up. Research from the National Literacy Trust (2011) indicates that, of pupils sampled, 33.6% of those who *'did not enjoy reading at all'* had below expected reading levels, while 97% of those who enjoyed reading were at or above expected reading levels.

Reluctant readers often struggle with 'getting into a book'. It takes a couple of chapters to get hooked and weaker readers are more likely to give up. Developing pupils' enjoyment of reading and their reading stamina is crucial. Having somebody to read to and / or who can join in by reading parts is a big help.

A 'reading buddy' scheme is an effective route to developing independent reading skills. This usually involves older pupils helping younger pupils with their reading, eg Sixth Form boys – who are often seen as 'cool' – listening to Year 8 reluctant readers; or Year 5's sharing a story they've written for Year 1's. Try to schedule paired reading once or twice a week. Ensure there is a comfortable area for reading and a simple system for checking progress.

Books for boys

All staff need some ideas about books to suggest to reluctant readers. More boys than girls are reluctant readers. Authors popular with both sexes, but particularly boys, include:

- Anthony Horowitz, particularly the *Alex Rider* series
- Robert Muchampre, *The Cherub* series (Book 1 – The Recruit)
- Philip Pullman, particularly the *Northern Lights* series
- Robin Jarvis, *The Deptford Mice* series
- Charlie Higson, *Young Bond* series
- Eoin Colfer, *Artemis Fowl* series
- Steve Bowkett's books, such as *The Frankenstein Steps and Other Adventures*
- Alan Gibbons' books such as *Shadow of the Minotaur*
- Terry Deary, *Horrible Histories*

Pupils are interested in what their teachers enjoyed reading at school. Don't be afraid to share your favourites and to seek opportunities to connect what you are currently teaching with books, both fiction and non-fiction.

Use of the library / resource centre

Schools that have attractive reading areas and resources are more likely to have motivated readers. Good reading resource centres have:

- Knowledgeable and interested specialist school librarians who are keen to recommend
- Pupils as 'library' helpers / monitors
- Good induction programmes and targeted sessions at key times – eg highlighting location of revision books in Year 10 or running study skills sessions
- Good links with teachers in different subject areas – e.g. asking them for recommendations and stocking books and resources that will be useful to their courses
- Exciting and attractive stock, including audio, dvds, periodicals and magazines to encourage *all* readers
- Regular events to entice pupils into the library and making it an attractive place to be. These could be chess clubs, homework clubs or reading groups
- Information about 'next steps', for example leaflets on 'Great Thrillers', 'Stories about School', 'Gripping Reads for Boys', etc that have been collated from suggestions by students
- Pupil surveys about reading and what would encourage them to read more
- Links with local libraries and library services to encourage reading at home

Pass on the passion – involve parents

Pupils spend much more time at home than they do at school. At home they have free time. Imagine the improvements in reading if all pupils spent just an hour a day enjoying some private reading?

Many schools run information evenings for parents about simple things they could do to boost pupils' reading and explaining *why* this is so important. An evening might include:

- A short practical presentation covering the importance of reading
- Guidance on selecting books and information about school and local libraries
- Information about suitable texts and reading lists
- Guidance on hearing your child read

The 'reading evening' could be a special event or a short presentation held when parents are already in school, say on a parents' evening. Invite a local bookseller to host a stand (make sure you pass on your recommended list in advance!).

Encouraging independent reading

If pupils are to become confident, capable, independent readers they need plenty of practice. That means opportunities for private reading at home and at school and tracking this.

How about having the whole school reading every Wednesday tutor time? Teachers and librarians will need to help reluctant readers select books they will enjoy; it is very dispiriting if you can't independently read most of the book you have chosen.

One primary head shares this simple tip:

> 'We use the 'five finger method' to decide whether a novel is appropriate independent reading material. Count the number of words on a single page that a child can't read, and if there are more than five it will be too difficult. For older pupils, work with roughly 5% - if a child struggles with more than 5% of words, the book will be too frustrating to read.'

This is a useful advice to give to parents who sometimes struggle to help their children select suitable books.

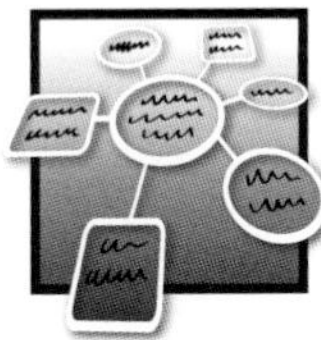

Note Making

Notes and literacy

Giving a training session in a Sixth Form College, I was surprised when the tutors complained that many 'A' Level pupils were unable to make good notes. Some of the weaknesses they cited included:

- Lack of basic organisation of notes and folders (particularly boys)
- Inability to distinguish the important facts from the trivial
- Illegible notes (particularly boys)
- Nonsense notes – both unstructured and meaningless
- Over zealous note making – particularly an issue with under confident girls whose notes are longer than the original text and are mainly copied out

Those who can produce effective notes have a great advantage over those who can't. Good notes can cement understanding, underpin revision, and inform planning and writing. This section will focus on strategies for developing the skills needed for making notes that support reading and writing across the curriculum.

Note well

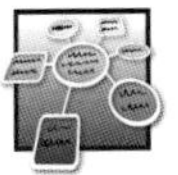

Within the context of literacy, there are two main aims in developing competent note making:

1. To **improve reading skills**.
2. To help with **organising ideas** leading to **better writing**.

Concentrating here on note making for reading we need to think about what outcome we want. We might be:

- Asking pupils to read a large amount of material from various different sources – internet and text based – skimming across a wide range to pick out important parts
- Reading shorter, but very dense, difficult texts and understanding and retaining the information for use at a later date

Do you teach pupils how to research information and record it in a helpful way? Or do you just hope for the best? One teacher asked pupils to research earthquakes and was surprised to received thirty printed out pages of Wikipedia and internet 'notes' – completely unassimilated by the pupil.

Improving research and note making skills

Setting up research and note making skills successfully might involve:

- Discussing with the pupils want they want to find out
- Collecting and posing good questions (see page 72 reading section)
- Discussing how the research will proceed
- Arranging some training with the school librarian on research skills
- Explaining how to avoid misleading information on the internet
- Issuing a number of pre-selected texts and getting them to do the research from these, perhaps a text with hyperlinks and list of resources
- Giving out guidance sheets, charts, writing frames to focus their recording of research
- Getting pupils to self- and peer-review the effectiveness of the research and methods

Summarising and re-presenting

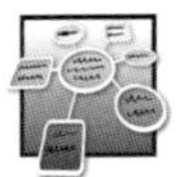

Note making for reading is about the ability to **summarise** and **re-present** information in your own words. To do this successfully you need to be able to understand what you have read before you make your notes.

Many students go wrong because they rush into writing notes without having processed or understood what they've read. They are then surprised and perplexed when they look back over their notes to find that they don't make sense.

Train pupils to ask questions about what they are reading as they go. Encourage them to re-read, look up definitions for words and explore parts that they do not understand **before** they commence making notes.

CASE STUDY

One teacher gets her class at the end of each session to summarise in only ten words the 'essence' of the lesson. Pupils go back to the start of their work (where they have left space next to the heading and date) and record their summary in green pen. This technique helps pupils to reflect and allows the teacher to understand what has been learnt during the lesson. All students have a handy summary of each lesson to refer to at a later date.

Visual devices and shorthand

Once pupils understand that they need to get the gist of something and know the key points in order to write coherent notes, you can help them further:

- Display some pages from revision books. Discuss with the class which they find the most effective and why? Discuss the use of space, heading, colour, and other visual devices to make meanings clear to the reader
- Make sure you model these devices when *you* make notes. Discuss with the class when it is helpful to use, eg colour to group or highlight points; headings to mark off sections; underlining for emphasis; bullets for lists; boxes for sections; arrows to make links; etc. These techniques help pupils both to process and memorise information
- Give advice on using helpful abbreviations to facilitate writing at speed. In history lessons, using govt, parl, K. Q. PM instead of government, parliament, King, Queen and Prime Minister can save a lot of time

Structuring notes

Teach pupils that there are different ways of recording and structuring their notes depending on purpose and context. Sometimes notes are personal aide memoirs; other times they will need to be viewed and understood by others. This will influence the choices they make.

So now they've got the gist of what they've read; they know the key points; they have some shorthand techniques. Next they have to **interpret** what they've been reading.

One way to do this is by **re-presenting** the information in a different or simpler form, eg turning fairly dense prose into a mind map, diagram or picture. You might want to provide pupils with a chart or table to fill in or get them to transform instructions with many steps into a flow chart. Giving them the structures first is important in modelling good note making.

Get pupils involved in thinking about their note making choices. What do they think would be the best way to distil information about a project?

Networked notes

In the *Learning to Learn Pocketbook* Tom Barwood explains the power of 'networked notes' (graphic organisers) for absorbing, organising and reviewing information and, indeed, for generating new ideas: *'The aim is to move away from making notes in a conventional way and to look at ideas from different angles...'*

The Herring Bone is a good note-making tool for explaining processes, recording time-lines or structuring ideas for essays.

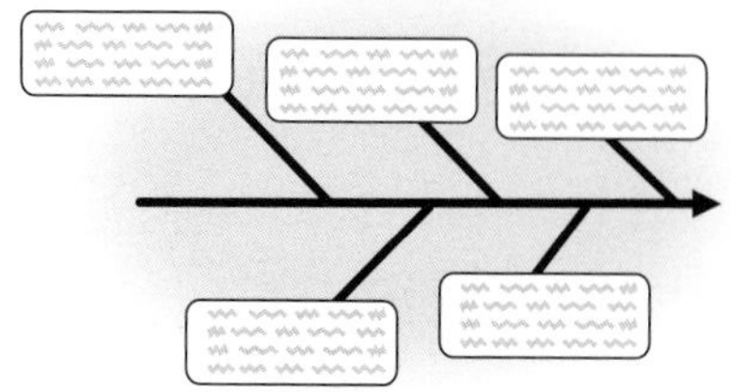

Herring Bone

Networked notes

The following all help pupils to gather and sort information and to think about the relationship between ideas. Introducing colour adds another helpful visual dimension.

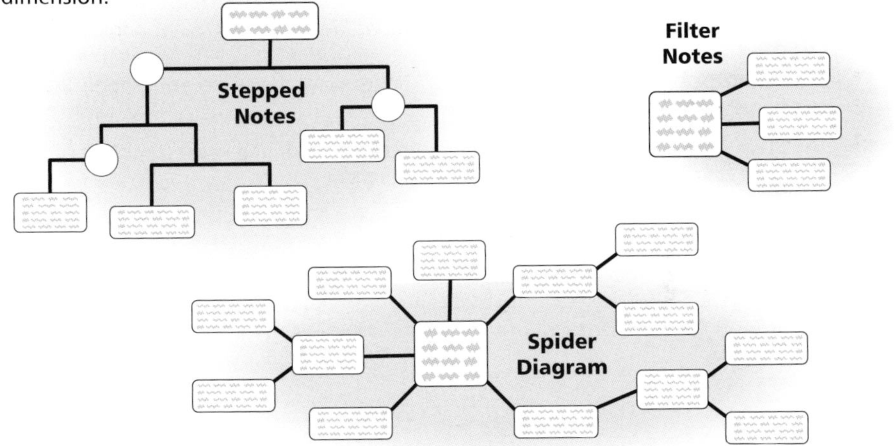

Stepped Notes

Filter Notes

Spider Diagram

Paper and online resources

There is a huge variety of paper and online ways to record information in note form. It's worth running some whole year-group sessions to familiarise pupils with the different tools available.

Two useful free online resources

- Mind42 http://mind42 – a browser based online mind mapping application that can be used alone or collaboratively
- The Brain. Free edition http://www.thebrain.com – a 'digital brain' that lets you 'organise and find everything the way *you* think'.

Two excellent books on visual tools

- *Thinking Skills and Eye Q: Visual Tools for Raising Intelligence* by Oliver Caviglioli et al.
- *Visual Tools for Transforming Information into Knowledge* by David Hyerle

Top tips for success

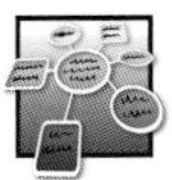

- Get pupils to review their notes from a previous lesson. Can they talk for five minutes about the previous lesson just from a page of notes? If so, the notes are effective
- When discussing a topic, explain and highlight to the class which are the important points so that they can be recorded – how do they signpost key information, such as word definitions?
- Get the class to decide on the most appropriate format for their notes – summary, list, table, chart, spider diagram, etc
- Tell pupils how *you* use colour, symbols and layout to aid your note making
- Relate a story or incident to the class getting them to pick out the key parts. Do they all agree on the main points?
- Use the whiteboard and other resources to showcase and model good note making skills, making explicit the choices you are making
- Get pupils to look at, comment on and critique each others' notes. What is effective? What could be clearer?

Notes for writing

Note making for better writing is part of the planning process. It involves working out which points you want to make and then organising them in a coherent and logical way. It's a three-stage process:

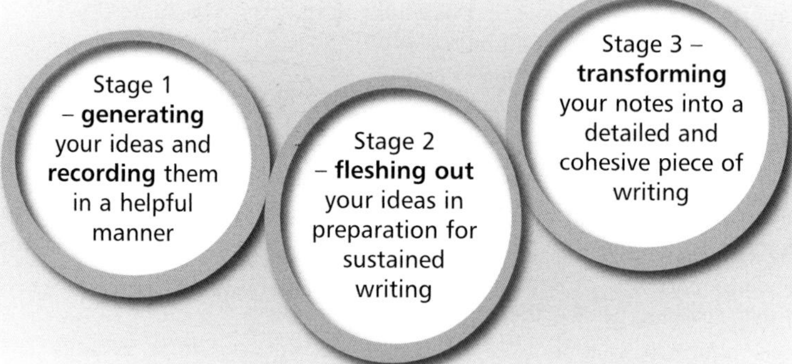

The writing process, including planning, is covered in the next chapter.

Write Better!

Writing skills

A group of adults were asked to log the different types of writing they undertook in a week. These were wide ranging, including various formal letters (complaining, informing, persuading, advising, requesting), various job / housing / banking applications, informal emails and text messages, reports, power point presentations, notes for a speech, filling out various forms and completing a survey.

Whether or not these were written effectively will have influenced these people's careers, relationships, business ideas and reputations.

The ability to communicate well in writing is crucial in making our lives a success.

What's the issue with writing?

> '47% of employers say that they cannot get recruits with the communication skills they need'
>
> (Communication Trust funded by the DFE, 2011)

A colleague recently commented that her new admin. assistant had to be reminded to write in paragraphs and did not know how to address a formal letter.

Even students continuing in education lack some basic skills. A survey by Cambridge Assessment found that: *'60% of Higher Education Institutes are having to put on extra courses in literacy / numeracy.'* (The Independent 3rd April 2012) Students are unprepared for academic writing and some struggle to express themselves clearly.

We make assumptions about people by their ability to communicate and the presentation of their work. By helping our pupils reach a good standard of written communication, we are ensuring that they have the best chance of securing employment and success in later life.

This section looks at eight steps to improving pupils' writing; gives tools and classroom tips for supporting the writing process in all subjects; and suggests some whole school writing ideas for literacy co-ordinators to promote.

Improving writing – eight steps to success

Sometimes we will set pupils a task expecting them to just do it. However, if this is the norm we are not making the best use of all opportunities to improve pupils' written skills. Follow eight key steps to improve your pupils' writing

1 Engage them in the process

It is important to get pupils thinking about what they already know about the type of writing you require before they start. So if you want pupils to write a news report about the murder of Thomas Becket:

- Ask them to think in pairs about a list of 'ingredients' found in newspapers, such as headlines, summary paragraph, including 'who', 'what', 'where' and 'why'. What ingredients make this type of text special? (eg the use of a dramatic, captioned picture)
- Reinforce any specific terminology so pupils have the vocabulary to express themselves and are using a common language

By assessing their knowledge *before* you start, any misconceptions can be corrected. The lesson also builds on, rather than duplicating, their knowledge, eg they might already be proficient at writing newspaper articles from their studies in English.

Study an example

Good writers need to know what they are aiming for if they are to achieve success. To become better writers, your pupils need first to be perceptive and thoughtful readers. Before embarking on a writing task, always try to **show an example of the type of text you are asking for.**

If you ask pupils in Geography to write a leaflet promoting the local area, why do you specify a leaflet rather than a news article or formal essay? The forms of writing are very different and have different purposes. If you ask them to write in a specific form then you need to remind them of the 'ingredients' found in this type of writing and show a good example.

Showing pupils an exemplar need not be a huge effort. Newspaper articles are easily found online, or with a visualiser or scanner you can easily show some examples from another class or the real world. It is important to talk through what they notice about this type of text, so that the reading is active.

Plan for success – structure and format

Good writers plan their work – even if they often adapt or amend their plans.

Get pupils to think about the overall plan and format of their work. What should it look like on the page? One inspiring Literacy Co-ordinator gives groups 'blocked out' plans and asks them to think about the type of writing it might be. This helps them understand about the importance of headings, sentence lengths, paragraphs and other aspects of layout.

Look at the following text. What do you think it might be?:

<u>XXXXXXXXXXXXXXXXXXXXXXXXXXXXXXXXXXXXXXXXXXXXXXXX.</u>

<u>XXXXXXXXXXXXXXXX</u>

1.
2.
3.
4.

XXXXXXXXXXXXXXXXXXXXXXXXXXXXXXXXXXXXXXXXXXXXXXXXXXXXXXXXXXXXXXXXXXXXXXXXX
XXXXXXXXXXXXXXXXXXXXXXXXXXXXXXXXXXXXXXXXXXXXXXXXXXXXXXXXXXXXXXXXXXXXXXXXX
XXXXXXXXXXXXXXXXXXXXXXXXXXXXXXXXXXXX

Plan content and organisation

Once pupils have decided on the structure of their work, they will need to plan the content in more detail. Suppose they are writing a formal report arguing against a motorway being built on some countryside, they might:

- Produce a spider diagram listing all their initial ideas
- Add further detail and link ideas together

Some students might now be ready to start writing, but those who regularly forget to paragraph might write down each main topic idea on a sticky note, and arrange them in a logical order, with each post-it representing a new paragraph.

Planning in a format that allows them to move their ideas about is a good way of making pupils think and reflect on structure. Networked notes and visual tools as described in the previous chapter provide other useful planning structures.

Right words – language and register

Next, pupils need to consider language and vocabulary. Good teachers get pupils discussing this *before* they start writing, encouraging them to pay particular attention to the **purpose** of the task, the **audience** and the expected **level of formality**. These three things determine the **register** of the writing.

For example, if they are writing up a science experiment there are conventions to follow, such as writing in the passive rather than the active voice:

'The test tube was placed...' rather than *'I placed the test tube...'*

Remind your students of any specialist vocabulary they will need for their writing. It is good practice to display this so that the correct spelling is on hand and any common misconceptions or errors are dealt with in advance.

In real life students will often need to write formally. All too often they use 'text speak', slang or inaccurate grammar. One exam board complained that in a GCSE English exam where the task was to write a formal letter to their headteacher, candidates frequently opened with 'Hi'!

6 Talk first!

Get pupils talking *before* they start to write. Discussing ideas leads to better understanding. Talking first also gives individuals a chance to rehearse their arguments, positions and thoughts, which in turn increases their confidence and enthusiasm for written work. Working with a 'talk partner' is a good way of getting pupils to think about content and to extend and refine their ideas.

Individual mini white boards are useful tools for getting pupils to relax and draft out ideas. The temporary nature of writing on a 'wipe clean' board means that pupils can experiment with ideas, planning and sentence starters without feeling that anything has been set in stone. (Remind them to note down in their books their best ideas or improvements before they are rubbed off!)

Although mini white boards are commonly used in primary schools, Ofsted (*Improving Sciences in Colleges,* October 2011) mentions their effectiveness in a Sixth Form science lesson, and encourages all teachers to see their potential as a teaching resource.

Modelling and sharing

It really helps if we model the writing and reviewing process for pupils with our own work. When you write something on the board, do you reflect on it? It is a good habit to adopt.

It's helpful to do some shared writing to raise your pupils' awareness of writing as a process. You start writing and ask pupils for contributions:

You: *So I am going to start my essay with the sentence: 'Curley's wife is a soft character in 'Of Mice and Men'.... Can anyone think of any improvements?*

Ben: *I think 'weak' or 'marginalised' would be a better word than 'soft'.*

You: *Why is marginalised a better word choice?*

Ben: *'Soft' is too vague. 'Marginalised' makes her sound like she is left out of society as well as the ranch.*

Kate: *I would start with, 'Steinbeck presents Curley's wife as a marginalised character.'*

You: *Yes that's a lot better; it shows that the author has deliberately created her this way. So, 'Steinbeck presents Curley's wife as a marginalised character'... ... Now spend two minutes with your partner completing the next three sentences and then we'll share them.*

Read, review, refine!

To become successful writers, pupils need to be able to review and redraft their work. It can be useful, initially, to provide a checklist to help them 'key into' what you are looking for. In Geography, if they are writing a route description using a map, the list might include:

- Use correct geographical terms, eg *north, south, east, west* rather than *left / right*
- Refer to correct factual evidence from map, eg names of farms and exact locations
- Write in a logical, structured way using specific detail within sentences, eg: *'Go north up the hill past Streetfields Farm'*, rather than *'turn left out of the village'*
- Use a separate paragraph for each main idea

As pupils progress, promote independence by encouraging them to devise the checklist themselves. This ensures that they are really thinking about what they are trying to achieve.

Don't forget to give them time to amend, improve and correct their work so that redrafting has a real purpose and impact on their writing. Getting pupils to highlight where they have met the given criteria is also important, and developing peer partners to assess each others' work can be effective. For more detail on setting this up – see 'the X factor' chapter in the *Outstanding Lessons Pocketbook.*

Making connections

The eight steps outlined in the previous pages will help your pupils to develop independence and to master key elements of the writing process. Now let's look at some engaging techniques for overcoming common problems and sharpening up their writing skills.

Good writers understand that connectives are central to developing a line of argument and to making a piece of writing read smoothly. However, some pupils just 'throw in' connectives in inappropriate places. They need to know what connectives are for:

Cause and effect – *because, therefore, since, hence, due to, as a result of*

Contrast – *on the other hand, however, whereas, even though, unlike, despite, yet, otherwise, alternatively*

Emphasis – *especially, significantly, in particular, above all, most importantly*

Comparison – *equally, similarly, like, likewise, as well as*

Illustration – *for instance, namely, such as, for example*

Sequencing – *later, next, meanwhile, then, first, second, finally, in the first place*

Connect it!

The game 'Connect It' is an ideal starter activity that reinforces the use of connectives.

- Put each connective on different cards and make sets for pupils
- Give pupils a topic to discuss linked to the planned writing outcome, eg: *'Is it better to start a new business as a Sole Trader or as a Limited Company?'*
- Initial thoughts are collected on a herring bone diagram (see page 94) and could include, *'easier to run as you have sole ownership and control'; 'capital can be raised by selling shares; 'quick to set up'*, etc
- Pupils play in threes, dividing the cards between two of them. These two have to use the cards to develop their argument. The winner uses all their cards correctly and develops the best argument. The third pupil acts as a 'spotter' and interrupts if errors are made.

Person 1: *'One reason you might choose to be a sole trader is that it is very simple to set up.* ***However,*** *if you become a limited company it then exists in its own right.'*

Person 2: *'This can be an advantage, though, because private limited companies have limited liability.* ***Therefore,*** *you are not personally liable for any losses the company makes;* ***whereas*** *if you are a sole trader you are liable for any debts you incur.'*

Visually planning and verbally rehearsing ideas like this leads to better written outcomes.

Supporting weaker writers

1. **Facing the Fear.** Some pupils really struggle with written work. The blank page can appear incredibly intimidating. Support these pupils by introducing the task very carefully, perhaps as a series of mini steps, making clear what pupils need to do to achieve at each stage. (Some pupils even like a word target – *'300 words for your introduction'*.)

2. **Writing Frames** are useful for suggesting ways to start and organise writing. They might include sentence openings, and/or a sequence of paragraph topic sentences to help pupils scaffold their writing, eg: *'The most important factor in designing a marketing campaign is...'* Remember, though, a writing frame is an aid for pupils, and ultimately we need to promote independence. Pupils should be encouraged to develop their own frames and some may not need them at all.

3. **True Story.** One teacher had a class full of very reluctant writers with low self-esteem. They felt they were always failing. She started some lessons by giving them an exemplar section of work with errors to spot and elements to improve. They enjoyed finding the mistakes. Improving the work themselves really built up their confidence.

Spot silly mistakes

Pupils need to be skilled in drafting and redrafting their work. All too often they want to finish as quickly as possible. They hand in work to their teacher without reading it over carefully first. It is frequently full of careless errors that they could and should have spotted themselves.

Teaching pupils to proof-read and making sure they do so is essential.

Peer checking can also be helpful, particularly if the mistakes are the result of carelessness rather than misunderstanding. Partners check each other's work, with a particular focus, eg full stops and capital letters. Each person starts with a notional 20 credits. Every time their partner 'finds' and corrects a mistake they are deducted one credit! The pupil who spots most corrections is given some reward such as a merit or becomes class literacy champion!

Get set, get gel!

CASE STUDY

Kate was frustrated with her class. They persistently made silly mistakes. Exams were only a week away... She gave a different coloured gel pen to each pupil in the class and set them part of an exam paper to work on in silence for 15 minutes. Then the work was redistributed. Pupils had five minutes to make corrections and improvements to the other person's work. How could they raise the level? Had the writer made any obvious errors? Next, pupils continued writing the other person's essay for a further ten minutes. The work was again redistributed and improved as before. At the end of the session pupils were re-united with their initial work and the developments and improvements.

Why it worked? Pupils do make silly mistakes. Peer correcting makes them more alert to this and helps them see ways of improving their answers. Boys often raise their game once they realise their work is being peer marked, and all pupils enjoy having their writing returned to them after it has been corrected. They also get the chance to see a range of different responses. A good discussion can be had at the end of the lesson where pupils feed back on common mistakes and identify the best qualities in the writing they looked at.

Tip: This technique also works brilliantly with any type of writing in primary school.

Writing Wheel

A useful tool to help pupils self- or peer-assess writing is my Writing Wheel. It covers the key components of effective writing. You can also use it to set specific targets for pupils and to chart their progress. There's a free A4 example under 'literacy resources' at www.bentley-davies.co.uk.

All these aspects are needed to get your target grade. Rate each section from 1 (*Really good – with a range of good examples*) to 5 (*Not present*). Where are your strengths? What do you need to work on?

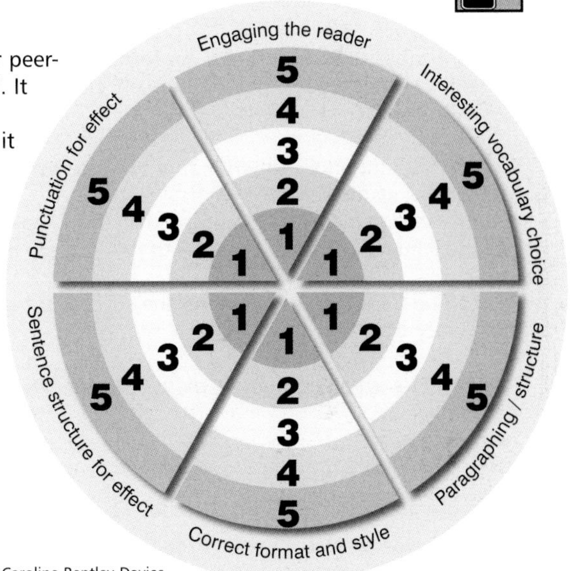

Engaging the reader 5 4 3 2 1

Interesting vocabulary choice 1 2 3 4 5

Paragraphing / structure 1 2 3 4 5

Correct format and style 1 2 3 4 5

Sentence structure for effect 1 2 3 4 5

Punctuation for effect 5 4 3 2 1

Writing in different subjects

Different subjects have different concerns when they set a written task. Subject content is clearly the top priority in many cases, but we also need to reinforce good literacy skills.

If you are asking pupils to write up a full account of a visit to a Catholic church in RE, then as well as the subject-specific information, it would be helpful to remind them to: write in sentences, to paragraph their work, and to reinforce any whole school or individual literacy targets – such as using accurate punctuation.

This can be done by clearly stating the success criteria for a piece of work, including the literacy objective, eg:

Task: *To write up an account of the visit to the Catholic Church.*

Success criteria:

- To include specific detail about what was seen and how it is used in worship
- To use accurate terminology to describe parts of the church
- (Literacy Objective) To write in full sentences and paragraphs

Writing is fun!

Good Literacy Co-ordinators also encourage writing for fun. This might take the form of creative writing clubs, arranging writing competitions, meeting authors and celebrating pupils' writing. There is a huge range of exciting possibilities.

Schools I have visited have:

- Set up surprises and simulations, for example transforming a classroom into a 'crime scene', getting pupils to become detectives to inspire writing linked with science lessons
- Created messages and artefacts from 'aliens' who have landed on the school field and want to find out about the school, inspiring 'live' news reporting and articles
- Sent the class emails or letters from their class teddy bear who is travelling the world and asking them questions about school
- Written books and resources for a real audience, such as story books for younger pupils or letters and presentations to adults about real concerns. Year 1 pupils completed a project about 'people who help us in school'. They took digital photographs of chosen adults from caretakers to teaching assistants, used a computer to write about them and then gave a presentation to parents and staff. It was very motivating!

Writing for real

Pupils make much more effort with their writing if they know it is for a specific purpose and will be read by a real audience. Aim for this as often as possible – sometimes it can involve just 'tweaking' a task. Instead of getting your pupils to write a speech about whether they should wear school uniform – ask them to write a letter to the Head of Year which they can actually deliver (and ask for a response!).

Even if you are producing something that does not have a 'real' audience you could get one involved. If students are producing a leaflet about their local area, invite a member of the Tourist Information Office to talk to them about it, or ask if the leaflets could be displayed in the Office.

Real Purpose = Task Valued
+ Additional Effort from Pupils

Encouraging pupils who don't like writing

One school held a special 'Writing Workshop' for a group of disaffected Year 8 boys who 'hated writing'. They invited an author of ghost stories along to run it. Initially the pupils worked in small self-selected friendship groups to make them feel secure about the challenging tasks they were asked to complete. Group work and competition inspired them.

Activities that 'hooked' pupils involved them: verbally discussing pictures before writing, studying samples of exciting texts in groups and feeding back what was effective about them. Pupils had to select five wrapped up 'mystery' articles per group. Bus tickets, foreign coins, an old piece of pottery, a rusty key, and a distinctive button provoked animated discussion. In their groups they had to create an exciting story opening that could be told to others using these items.

Eventually, after much discussion and looking at sample quality texts, each pupil produced a gripping, finely crafted story opening. Many of them said it was the best writing they had ever done and many continued at home, working them up into complete stories. These were word processed into 'books' that pupils could celebrate and take home.

Using ICT to encourage writing

There is a vast range of ICT opportunities that can give pupils a real platform for their work. Many schools have had success with the following:

School newspapers and magazines. One school has a pupil reporting team and a committee of Sixth Formers who oversee the paper's layout and production. A staff member just checks over the final draft before publication.

Wikis. These are websites that users can easily add to or amend. One teacher started one on a French exchange so that parents could be updated about what was happening on the trip and read accounts of the day visits. Pupils were motivated to contribute because they knew it would be read and they had a limited time to write their responses. Levels of access can be restricted to certain groups or individuals.

Blogs. Many schools start up class blogs and use them to display projects or stories. Check out The Literacy Shed (www.literacyshed.com) for schools' blogs from around the world. Seek advice from your IT co-ordinator about creating your own blog and about issues relating to editing rights. Ensure that you have your headteacher's permission before creating any online platforms relating to your school.

Literacy Checklist

LAC audit for everyday lessons

It is helpful as a class teacher or department head to audit your teaching of LAC. Take a look at the questions that follow and consider how effectively you and your department are implementing the different elements of LAC.

1 = Needs attention

2 = Developing

3 = Fully in place

Look at the areas you feel secure about and then consider those that are less developed. This will help pinpoint some personal targets and could provide a starting point for discussion with your literacy co-ordinator, literacy working party or line manager.

The checklist can also be used by literacy co-ordinators, in conjunction with lesson observations and sampling pupils' books, to identify whole school priorities and staff training needs.

Self-audit

Some features of LAC	Current Practice
1. Do you highlight and teach pupils strategies to remember key vocabulary?	1 2 3
2. Are dictionaries and thesauruses available? Do pupils refer to them?	1 2 3
3. Do you correct pupils' spelling, punctuation and grammar where appropriate?	1 2 3
4. Do you expect pupils to amend and learn from their corrections and do you give them time to do this, following up on corrections either yourself or via a teaching assistant?	1 2 3
5. When setting a written task do you address **how** it should be written, as well as what the content should be?	1 2 3
6. Do you use 'talk for learning'? (eg 'talk partners' to discuss and plan ideas.)	1 2 3
7. Do you discuss with pupils correct use of standard English and model good practice, eg challenging inappropriate register and correcting grammatical errors such as, '*we was*'?	1 2 3
8. Do you give pupils opportunities to take part in a range of formal and informal speaking and listening activities?	1 2 3

Self-audit

Some features of LAC **Current Practice**

9. Do you teach pupils how to make effective notes, and reinforce this in lessons?

10. Are you following the school's marking policy for literacy?

11. Is it having a positive effect on pupils' progress and skills and enhancing the quality of teaching and learning in your classroom?

12. Does pupils' work show evidence of them making improvements in areas of literacy?

13. Do you make good use of exemplars/use a visualiser to show pupils what they are aiming for?

14. Do you promote reading for pleasure in your department?

15. Do parents know how they can help pupils with the literacy demands of your subject? Do you provide guidance and resources?

16. Are you aware of which pupils have specific literacy issues/IEPs? Are you addressing these /asking for advice?

Finally, make a note of the following:

- What aspects of LAC do you think you / your area is doing well in?
- What further advice, support, training or resources would help you / your department / your school tackle literacy issues more effectively?

Recommended reading

The Literacy Toolkit: Improving Students' Speaking, Listening, Reading and Writing Skills by Amanda Sara. Published by Crown House, 2009

Literacy Across the Curriculum: Making it Happen by Julia Strong. Published by Collins Educational, 2001

Literacy in the Secondary School by Maureen Lewis & David Wray. Published by David Fulton, 2000

Talk for Writing Across the Curriculum by Pie Corbett and Julia Strong. Published by Open University Press, 2011

Story Journeys (9 story packs improving writing KS2,) by Jane Considine. Published by Val Sabin Publications and Training

Dyslexia Pocketbook by Julie Bennett. Published by Teachers' Pocketbooks, 2006

EAL Pocketbook by Alice Washbourne. Published by Teachers' Pocketbooks, 2011

Handwriting Pocketbook by Julie Bennett. Published by Teachers' Pocketbooks, 2007

Moving English Forward: Action to raise standards in English. Survey on literacy issues (Ofsted, 2012, ref. 110118)

Reading by Six: How the best schools do it. (Ofsted, 2010, ref. 100197) www.ofsted.gov.uk.

Literacy websites and resources

www.literacyshed.com (The Literacy Shed). Brilliant website offering lots of creative ideas to stimulate writing and reading; links to exciting digital resources. Explore different 'sheds' linked to different genres and writers. Attractive, fun and very useful.

www.worldbookday.com a range of good ideas and interactive suggestions for promoting reading on this special occasion and all year around. It has links to Readathon.

www.readathon.org a popular charity and extra-curricular reading event.

www.oxforddictionaries.com free online resources for teaching pupils about words and consolidating their understanding of many aspects of literacy.

www.gl-assessment.co.uk Literacy and numeracy testing, resources and assessments. Tel: 0845 6021937.

www.oxfordsecondary.co.uk (Oxford University Press)
Rollercoasters – series of novels and reading packs for ages 11-14 (eg *Trash* by Andy Mulligan and *Sky Hawk* by Gill Lewis.) Free online support and lesson plans.
Oxford Playscripts – including *Frankenstein,* adapted by Philip Pullman and *War Horse* adapted by Nick Stafford.

www.pearsonschoolsandfecolleges.co.uk/secondary/literature/11-14 The 'Heroes' series, novels and plays aimed at KS3 boys. Check out their 'library pack' of twelve titles.

Organisations for literacy and promoting reading

The National Association for the Teaching of English www.nate.org.uk – has a range of useful resources for purchase including the brilliant 'Rooted in Reading' passports. Members get various free publications crammed with great ideas.

Book Trust www.booktrust.org.uk – Independent educational charity working to promote books and reading with children and adults.

The National Literacy Trust www.literacytrust.org.uk – produces resources, research and hosts a fantastic website.

The National Literacy Association www.nla.org.uk – works with children who are underachieving in literacy. Resources and publications to support teachers and parents.

The Reading Agency www.readingagency.org.uk – useful links to their work in promoting reading with children and adults in a range of settings.

The National Centre for Language and Literature www.ncll.reading.ac.uk – University of Reading. Useful listing of contact details for authors, illustrators, poets and story tellers that can visit and run workshops in school.

About the author

Caroline Bentley-Davies

Caroline Bentley-Davies has been an English Adviser for a Local Authority and an Inspector. She has run training for thousands of teachers on aspects of outstanding lessons, Literacy Across the Curriculum and how to improve English GCSE results.

She teaches demonstration lessons and runs master classes on creative writing for pupils from primary age to A Level. She has written a range of popular GCSE English text books and runs English GCSE revision classes for A/A* pupils and those on the C/D borderline. For information about her training, consultancy and other books visit Caroline's website: www.bentley-davies.co.uk or follow her on twitter @RealCBD

Caroline also runs Literacy Across the Curriculum training courses with Osiris Education (www.OsirisEducation.co.uk) as well as training days directly with individual schools.